Grade 5 Skillbook

Grade 5 Math Skillbook
©2000 by TREND enterprises, Inc.
KidSparks™ is the registered trademark of TREND enterprises, Inc.

All rights reserved. No part of this publication may be reproduced or transmitted in any form or by any means, electronic or mechanical, including photocopying, recording, or any information storage and retrieval system, without permission from the publisher. For additional information, write to TREND enterprises, Inc., P.O. Box 64073, St. Paul, MN 55164 U.S.A.

Printed in the United States of America

Julie A. Fisher—Writer
Juli A. Gordon—Editor
Mark Engblom—Designer

ISBN 1-889319-68-6

10 9 8 7 6 5 4 3 2

Out of This World

Skill: Writing large numbers

Write the numerical form of the numbers in each sentence. Then find the numbers in the puzzle (numbers may run forwards, backwards, or diagonally.)

1. The moon's average distance from the earth is three hundred eighty four thousand kilometers. _____

2. Mercury's average distance from the sun is fifty-seven million, nine hundred ten thousand kilometers. _____

3. The average distance from Earth to the sun is one hundred forty-nine million, six hundred thousand kilometers. _____

4. Neptune's average distance to the sun is four billion, four hundred ninety-seven million, seventy thousand kilometers. _____

5. Jupiter's polar diameter is one hundred thirty-three thousand, seven hundred eight kilometers. _____

6. The temperature at the center of the sun is fourteen million degrees. _____

7. Scientists theorize that our sun was born four billion, six hundred million years ago. _____

4	1	0	1	5	7	8	1	5	4
1	4	9	3	0	0	0	3	7	6
4	9	9	3	0	0	0	3	9	0
0	6	0	7	0	0	0	7	1	0
0	0	0	0	0	0	0	0	0	0
0	0	8	6	0	7	0	8	0	0
0	0	6	9	0	0	0	0	0	0
0	0	4	0	4	0	9	0	0	0
0	0	0	8	0	0	7	0	0	0
1	3	3	0	9	7	5	7	0	0

Mind Stretchers

1. Round $7,563 to the hundreds place. _____
2. A pentagon has ___ sides.
3. 7___5 + ___42___ = 3208
4. 2, 4, 8, ___, ___, ___

In the Shade

Skills: Prime numbers, Composite numbers

Remember: A prime number has only two factors, 1 and itself. Composite numbers are not prime. 1 is composite, not prime, because it only has one factor.

Shade in the prime numbers to create a mathematical dessert.

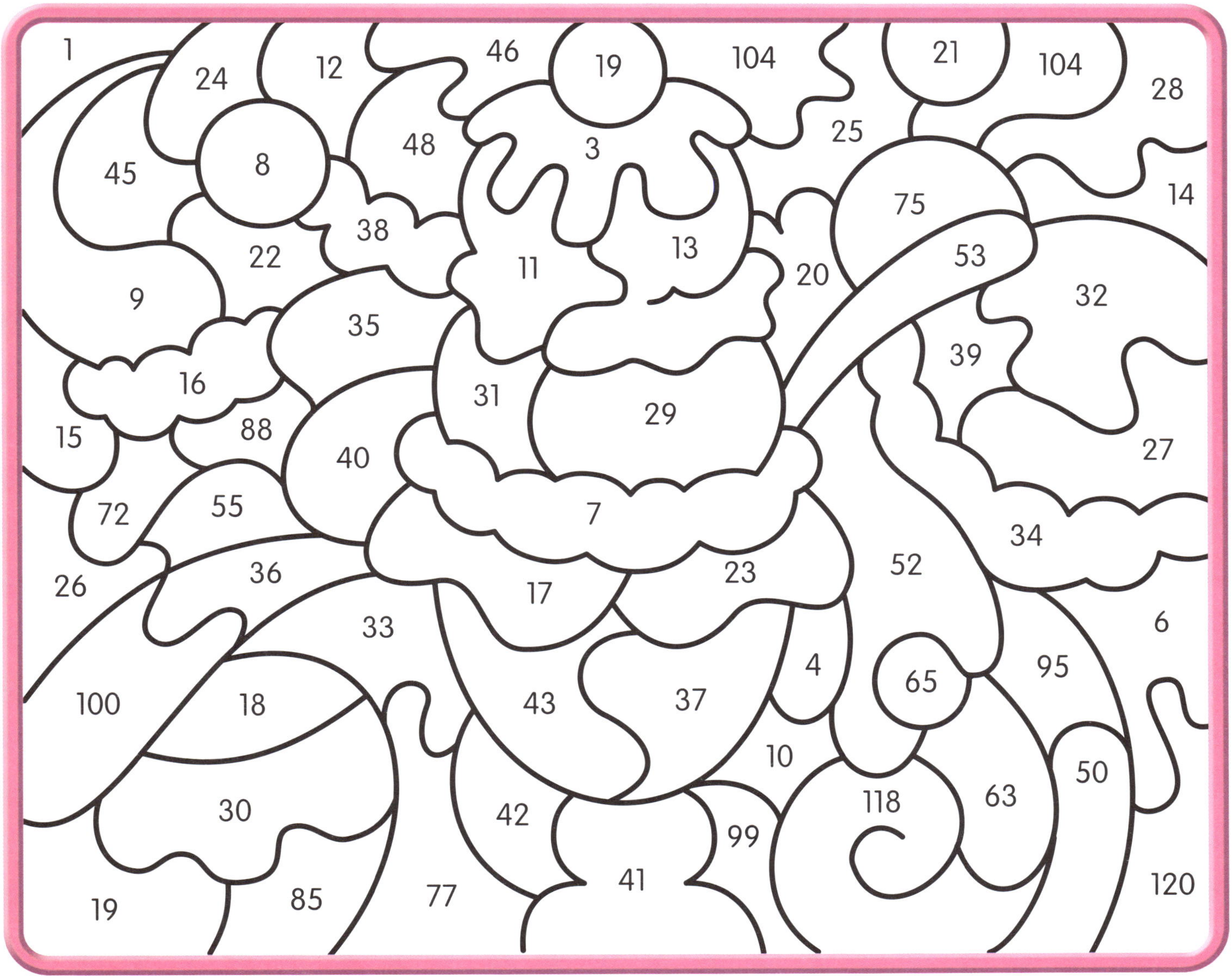

MIND stretchers

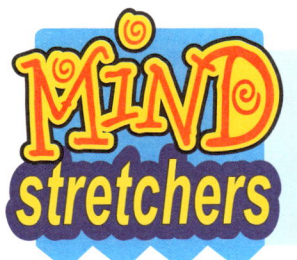

1. 10 x 9 x 8 x 7 x 6 x 5 x 4 x 3 x 2 x 1 x 0 = ________

2. What time is it? ____________

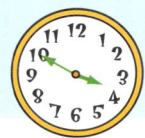

3. $\frac{7}{10}$ ($<$ $>$) $\frac{3}{10}$

4. The only even prime number is ___.

Tan-fastic

Skills: Perimeter, Area, Tangrams

Find the perimeter and area of each rectangle or square.

Remember:
Perimeter = sum of the sides.
Area = length x width.

	Perimeter	Area
1		
2		
3		
4		
5		
6		
7		

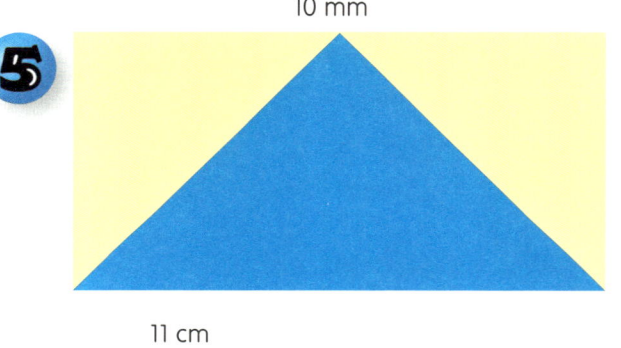

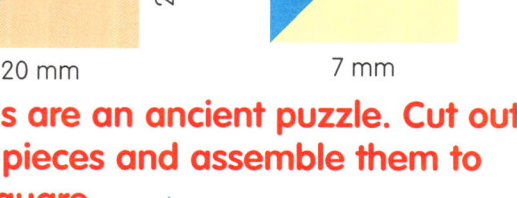

Tangrams are an ancient puzzle. Cut out the blue pieces and assemble them to form a square.

remember: Complete and check the previous page before cutting this page.

Challenge: Find the area of the shaded triangles!

1. There are ___ days in the first four months of a non-leap year.
2. Estimate 83,840 + 51,225 _____
3. A rectangular prism has ___ faces.
4. 9 x 11 = 105 - _____

Math Skillbook

Pull Out the Average

Skill: Finding averages

For each set of numbers, one of the numbers is actually the average of all the other numbers in the set. Find the number that is the average for each set.

To find the average of 8, 5, 9, 10:
add 8 + 5 + 9 + 10 = 32 ; 32 ÷ 4 = 8

Numbers | Average

1. 12, 20, 10, 14
2. 2, 6, 9, 5, 8
3. 9, 5, 10, 8, 13
4. 12, 11, 10, 21, 1
5. 10, 18, 1, 8, 3
6. 5, 6, 7, 6, 5, 7
7. 15, 4, 9, 7, 14, 5

Mind Stretchers

1. $20.00 − $12.54 = _____

2. $\frac{1}{3}$ (< >) $\frac{1}{5}$

3. 3 days = ___ hours.

4. 124 × 2 = _____

A-Round the Rules

Skill: Circumference

Find the circumference of each circle to the nearest whole number. Use the π key on your calculator or use 3.14 for π.

Remember: Circumference = π × diameter or π × twice the radius.

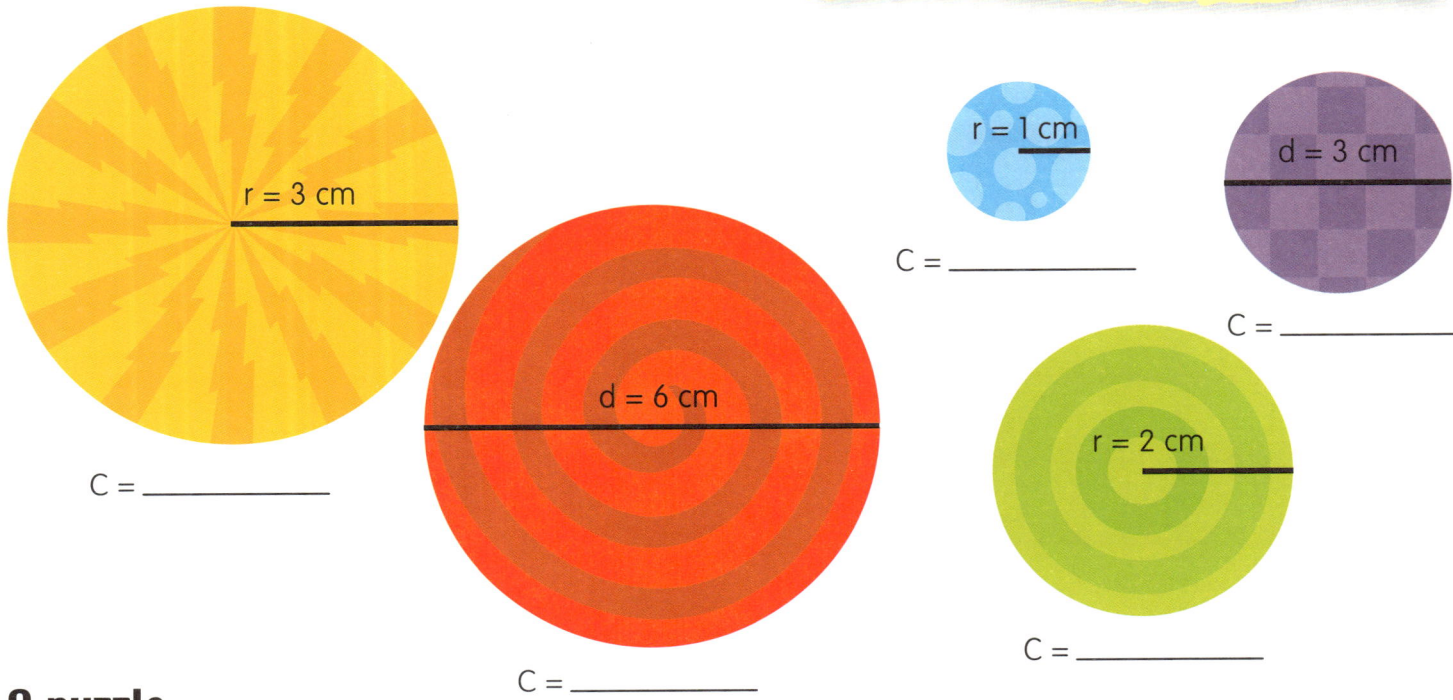

- r = 3 cm, C = _____
- d = 6 cm, C = _____
- r = 1 cm, C = _____
- d = 3 cm, C = _____
- r = 2 cm, C = _____

A puzzle

Cut out the five circles and the strip below. Place the circles in a pile on any x, with the largest circle on the bottom. Now move all the circles in the pile to another x following these rules:

1. You may only move one circle at a time.
2. You may never place a larger circle on a smaller one.

remember: Complete and check the previous page before cutting this page.

[strip with three X marks]

Mind stretchers

1. Round 2.65 to the nearest whole number. _____
2. ___4___ − 188 = 459
3. Each angle in a rectangle measures _____ degrees.
4. Write five thousand eight in digits. _____

Math Skillbook — ©2000 TREND enterprises, Inc.

Birthday Bonanza

Skill: Graphs and tables

The children at a birthday party were surveyed to find their favorite ice cream flavors. Use the graph to answer the questions.

1 How many children liked each of the flavors?

_____ chocolate   _____ vanilla   _____ strawberry

_____ cookies & cream   _____ mint   _____ bubble gum

2 Which flavor was most popular? Least?

Most _____   Least _____

3 How many more children liked vanilla than strawberry? _____

4 If each child only chose one flavor, how many children were at the party? _____

5 If each child chose more than one flavor, what is the smallest number of children that could have been at the party? _____

6 Change the graph by adding your favorite flavor(s).

The toys in the party favor box were counted. Complete the table and answer the questions.

1 What was the most common toy? _____

2 What was the least common toy? _____

3 How many more tops than flags were there? _____

4 Rings are worth 10¢, balls are worth 5¢, flags are worth 8¢, tops are worth 4¢, cars are worth 12¢, and patches are worth 9¢. How much is the entire chest full of toys worth? _____

5 If each of the 27 children gets one toy, how many children will get a top or a patch? _____

Toy	Tally	Total
Rings	////	
Balls	//// /	
Flags	//	
Tops	////	
Cars	///	
Patches	//// //	

Wheel of Factors

Skill: Greatest common factor

For each pair of numbers, find the Greatest Common Factor (GCF) and place that number in the outer circle.

Remember: The GCF is the largest number that can go into a pair or group of numbers evenly.

Example: Factors of 15 = 1, 3, 5, 15
Factors of 20 = 1, 2, 4, 5, 10, 20

The greatest common factor of 15 and 20 is 5.

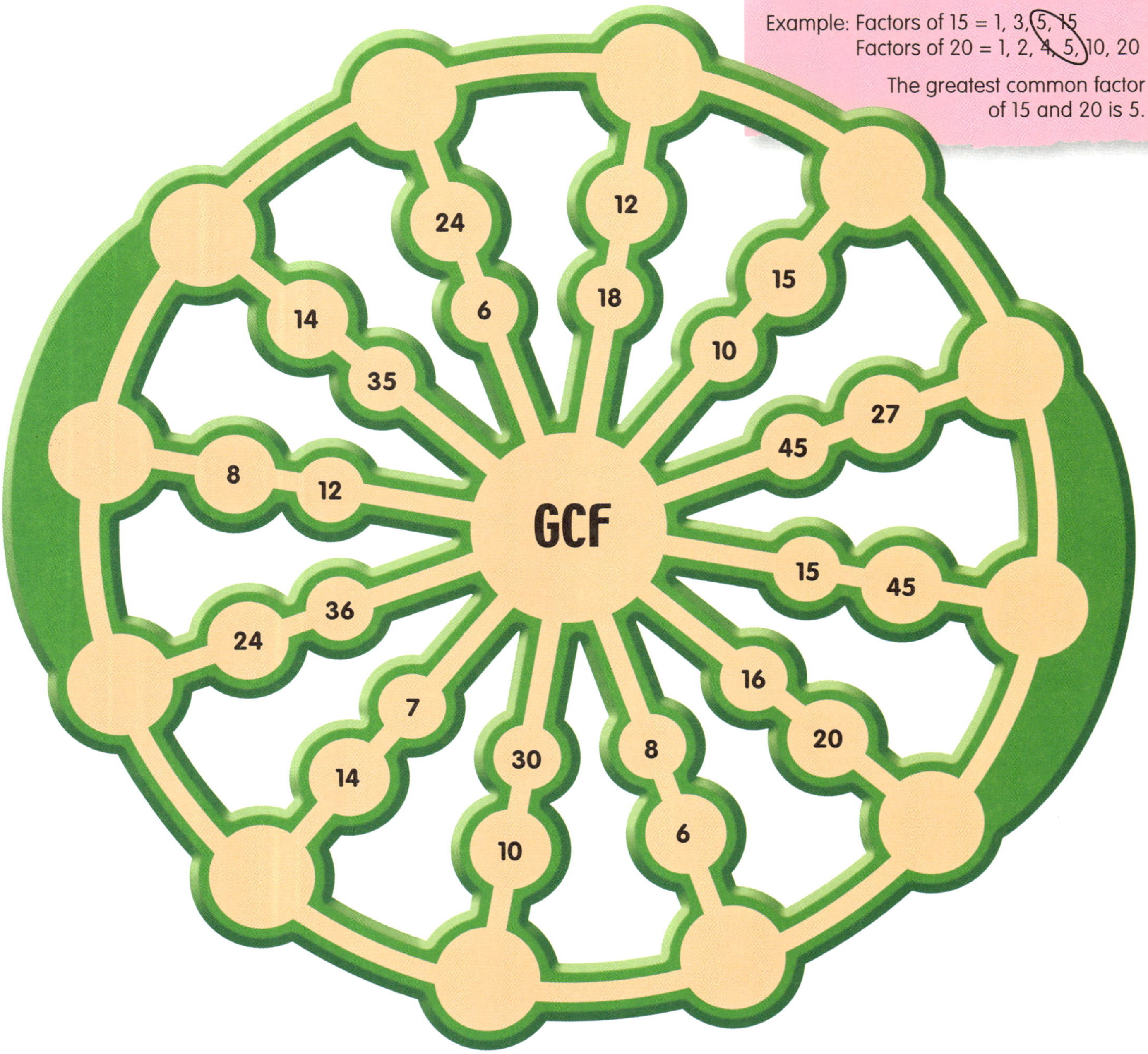

[Wheel diagram with pairs: 24 & 12, 6 & 18, 15 & 10, 45 & 27, 15 & 45, 16 & 20, 8 & 6, 30 & 10, 7 & 14, 24 & 36, 8 & 12, 14 & 35]

1. 40.2 + 136.5 = _____
2. (10,000 − 1,000) + (100 − 1) = _____
3. A hexagon has ___ sides.
4. Use 5, 9, and 7 to make the largest 3 digit number. _____

8

Math Skillbook © 2000 TREND enterprises, Inc.

Multiple Wheels

Skill: Least common multiple

For each pair of numbers, find the Least Common Multiple (LCM) and place that number in the outer circle.

Remember: The LCM is the smallest number that is a multiple of a pair or group of numbers

Example: The multiples of 5 = 5, 10, 15, 20, 25, 30, 35, 40…
The multiples of 6 = 6, 12, 18, 24, 30, 36, 42, 48…

The LCM of 5 and 6 is 30.

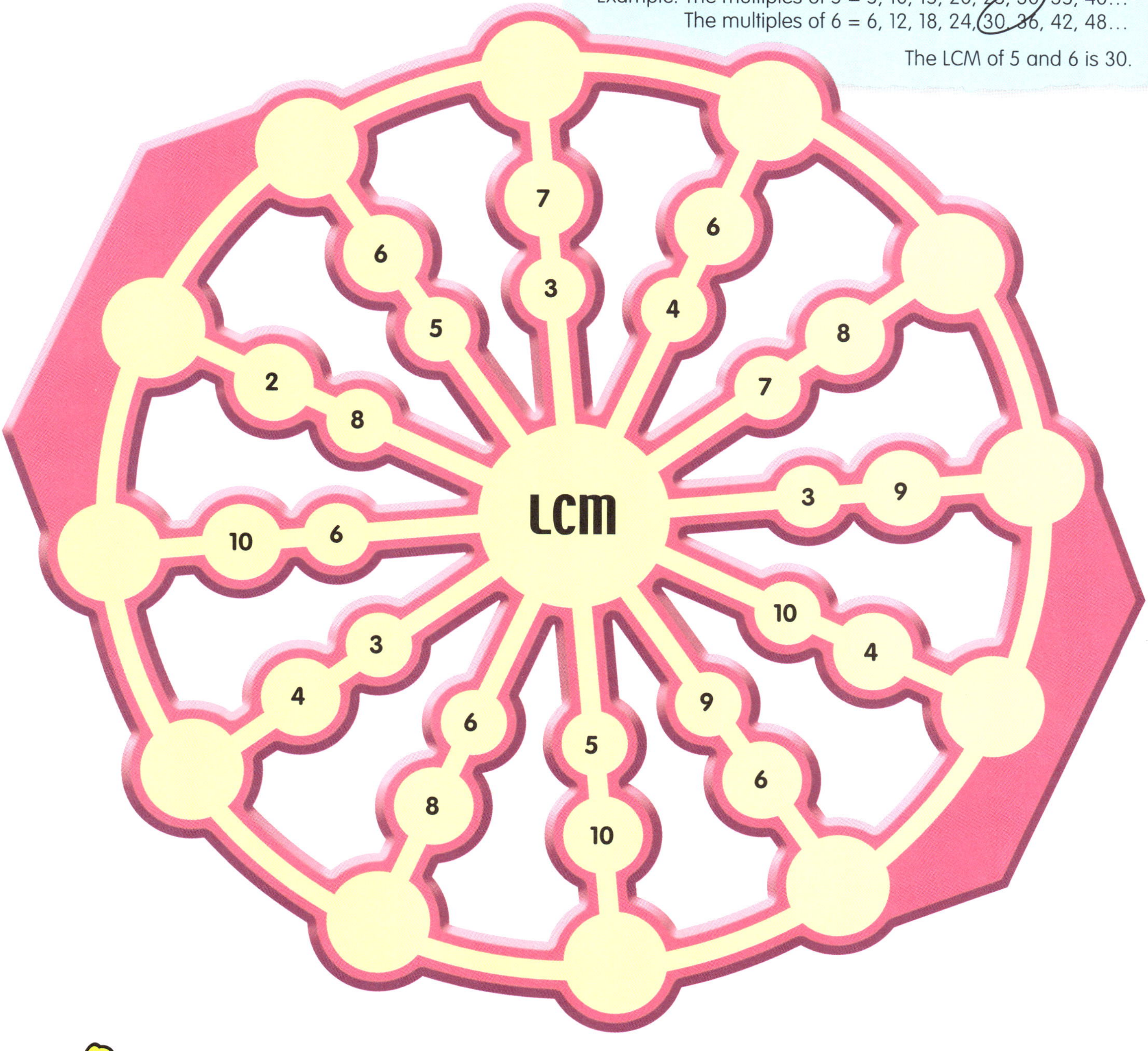

[Wheel pairs: 7 & 3, 6 & 4, 6 & 5, 8 & 7, 2 & 8, 3 & 9, 10 & 6, 10 & 4, 3 & 4, 9 & 6, 6 & 5, 8 & 10]

1. 9:30 P.M. to 7 A.M. is ___ hours.
2. $\frac{3}{4}$ of an 8 slice pizza is _____ slices.
3. $6.75 = ___ nickels
4. The sum of the first 4 prime numbers is _____ .

Line 'em Up

Skills: Ordering fractions, Equivalent fractions

Cut the diagram into nine square cards.
Use the cards in two ways:

 Make a fraction train: Use the fractions in the circles to line up the cards from the smallest fraction to largest.

 Heads and Tails: Match up the cards so that equivalent fraction heads and tails are touching side by side. When you are done, the cards will form a 3 x 3 square again.

remember: Complete and check the previous page before cutting this page.

1. 35 × 3 = _____

2. 32,781 − 9,442 = _____

3. List the factors of 12.
   _____

4. $\dfrac{1}{2} = \dfrac{}{8}$

Math Skillbook

©2000 TREND enterprises, Inc.

Reach for the Stars

Skill: Adding and subtracting fractions

Use the numbers in the diagram to solve each problem.

1.  $\dfrac{7 \times 1}{12 \times 1} = \dfrac{7}{12}$

 $\dfrac{1 \times 3}{4 \times 3} = \dfrac{3}{12}$

+ _____

$\dfrac{10}{12} = \dfrac{5}{6}$

2.  =

 =

− _____

3.  =

 =

+ _____

4.  =

 =

− _____

5.  =

 =

+ _____

6.  =

 =

− _____

7.  =

 =

− _____

8.  =

 =

+ _____

9. =

 =

+ _____

1. $3\tfrac{1}{2}$ hours = ___ minutes.

2. 12 × 4 = 100 − ___

3. $\dfrac{1}{6} + \dfrac{1}{6} =$ _____

4. 56.18 − 4.8 = _____

Gridlock

Skill: Multiplying fractions

Multiply the fractions and reduce the answer to lowest terms to complete the table.

x	$\frac{2}{3}$	$\frac{5}{7}$	$\frac{1}{6}$	$\frac{3}{4}$
$\frac{1}{2}$	$\frac{2}{6} = \frac{1}{3}$			
$\frac{4}{5}$				
$\frac{3}{8}$				
$\frac{2}{9}$				

Cut the puzzle out along the blue lines. Mix up the pieces. Try to put the pieces back together to form the square.

remember: Complete and check the previous page before cutting this page.

1. Reduce $\frac{20}{45}$ to its lowest terms. _____
2. If you run $\frac{1}{2}$ km each day for a week, you will have run _____ km.
3. Estimate 22 x 301 = _____
4. $\frac{3}{5} - \frac{1}{3}$ = _____

Pyramid Mystery

Skill: Adding and subtracting mixed numbers

Add and subtract the mixed numbers to fill in the pyramid. Start at the top and work down, following the lines in the pyramid.

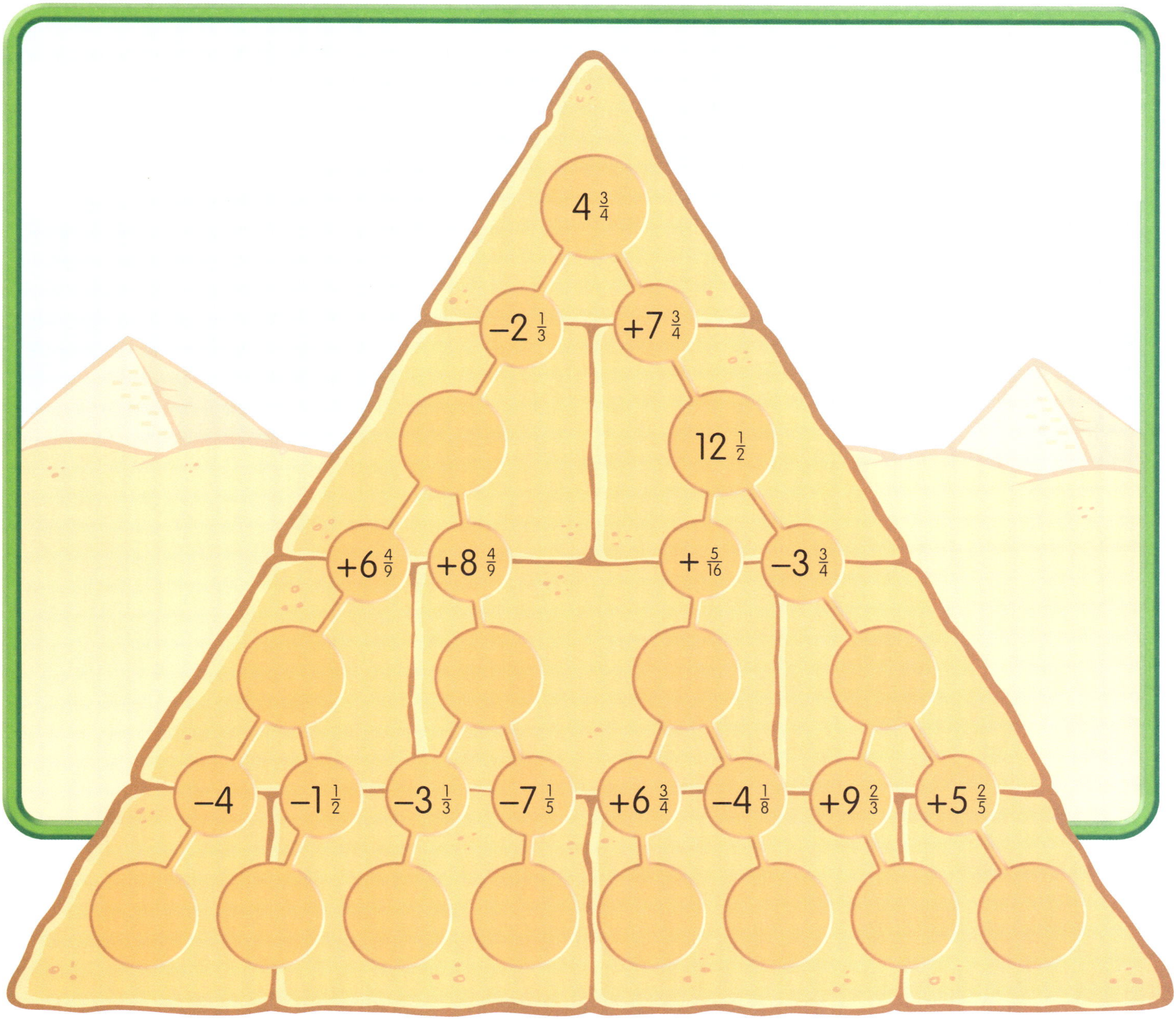

Top of pyramid: $4\frac{3}{4}$

Row 2: $-2\frac{1}{3}$, $+7\frac{3}{4}$

Row 3: (blank), $12\frac{1}{2}$

Row 4: $+6\frac{4}{9}$, $+8\frac{4}{9}$, $+\frac{5}{16}$, $-3\frac{3}{4}$

Row 5: (blanks)

Row 6: -4, $-1\frac{1}{2}$, $-3\frac{1}{3}$, $-7\frac{1}{5}$, $+6\frac{3}{4}$, $-4\frac{1}{8}$, $+9\frac{2}{3}$, $+5\frac{2}{5}$

Bottom row: (blanks)

Use the background for your work space.

1. 8.88 − 8.8 = _____

2. $12.75 = ___ quarters

3. Write one million five using digits.
   _____

4. $\frac{5}{9} + \frac{1}{9}$ = _____ .

13

Math Skillbook

©2000 TREND enterprises, Inc.

Around Times

Skill: Multiplying mixed numbers

Complete the spiral by filling in the blanks. The first one is done for you.

$3\frac{2}{3} \times 2\frac{2}{5} = 8\frac{4}{5} \times 3\frac{1}{8} = $

$\times \frac{1}{10} = $

$\times 2\frac{2}{7} = $

$\times 4\frac{2}{11} = $

$\times 1\frac{1}{5} = $

$\times \frac{3}{14} = $

$\times 1\frac{3}{1} = $

$\times 5\frac{1}{4} = $

$\times 2\frac{4}{23} = $

$\times \frac{1}{10} = $

Remember:

To change a mixed number into an improper fraction: multiply the whole number by the denominator, add the numerator to get a new numerator. The denominator stays the same.

$3\frac{5}{8}$

$3 \times 8 = 24 + 5 = 29$

$3\frac{5}{8} = \frac{29}{8}$

1. What is the sum of your birthday (month + day + year)? _____

2. 20 weeks = _____ days

3. School lasts from 8 A.M. to 3 P.M. What fraction of the day is that? _____

4. $1 - \frac{3}{5} = $ _____

Math Skillbook

©2000 TREND enterprises, Inc.

Answers

Math Grade 5

Page 2
Out of this World
1. 384,000
2. 57,910,000
3. 149,600,000
4. 4,497,070,000
5. 133,708
6. 14,000,000
7. 4,600,000,000

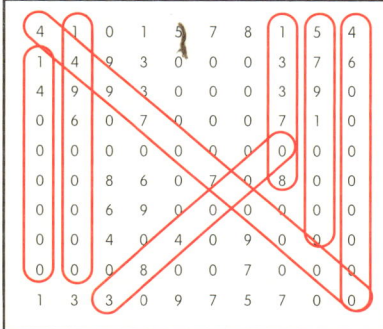

1. $7,600
2. 5
3. 7 _8_ 5 + _2_ 42 _3_ = 3208
4. 2, 4, 8, _14_, _22_, _32_

Page 3
In the Shade

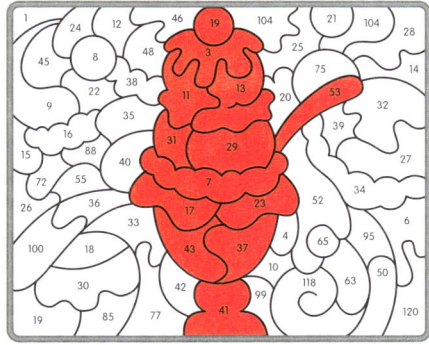

1. 0
2. 3:50
3. >
4. 2

Page 4
Tan-fastic

	Perimeter	Area
1.	32 m	64 m^2
2.	12.6 km	8.6 km^2
3.	18 km	18 km^2
4.	42 mm	98 mm^2
5.	30 mm	50 mm^2
6.	80 mm	400 mm^2
7.	44 cm	121 cm^2

Area of triangles
2. 8.6 km^2 6. 200 mm^2
3. 9 km^2 7. 60.5 cm^2
5. 25 mm^2

1. 120   3. 6
2. 130,000   4. 6

Page 5
Pull Out the Average
1. 14   5. 8
2. 6   6. 6
3. 9   7. 9
4. 11

1. $7.46   3. 72
2. >   4. 248

Page 6
A-Round the Rules
r = 3 cm   C = _18.84 cm_
d = 6 cm   C = _18.84 cm_
r = 1 cm   C = _6.28 cm_
r = 2 cm   C = _12.56 cm_
d = 3 cm   C = _9.42 cm_

Mindstretchers

1. 3   4. 5008
2. _6_ 4 _7_ − 188 = 459
3. 90°

Page 7
Birthday Bonanza
Favorite Ice cream Flavors
1. chocolate _4_   vanilla _5_
   strawberry _3_
   cookies & cream _4_
   mint _2_   bubble gum _3_
2. Most _vanilla_   Least _mint_
3. 2 children
4. 21 children
5. 5 children

Toys
1. Patches
2. Flags
3. 3
4. $2.05
5. 12

Toy	Tally	Total
Rings	IIII	4
Balls	ℋ I	6
Flags	II	2
Tops	ℋ	5
Cars	III	3
Patches	ℋ II	7

Page 8
Wheel of Factors

1. 176.7   3. 6
2. 9,099   4. 975

Answers

Math Grade 5

Page 9

Multiple Wheels

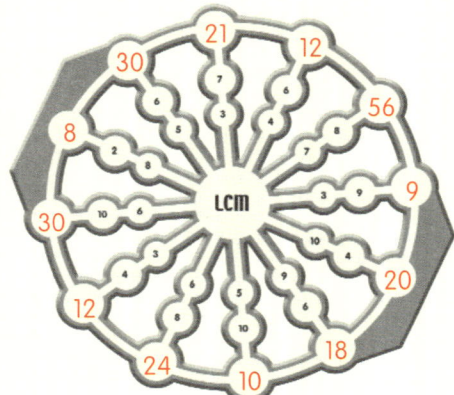

1. 9.5   3. 135
2. 6   4. 17

Page 10

Line 'em Up

1. Fraction Train

   $\frac{1}{6}$ $\frac{1}{4}$ $\frac{5}{12}$ $\frac{1}{2}$ $\frac{7}{12}$ $\frac{5}{8}$ $\frac{2}{3}$ $\frac{3}{4}$ $\frac{7}{8}$

2. Heads and Tails

1. 105
2. 23,339
3. 12 : 1,2,3,4,6,12
4. $\frac{1}{2} = \frac{4}{8}$

Page 11

Reach for the Stars

2. $\frac{3 \times 8}{5 \times 8} = \frac{24}{40}$
   $-\frac{1 \times 5}{8 \times 5} = \frac{5}{40}$
   $\overline{} \frac{19}{40}$

3. $\frac{2 \times 8}{3 \times 8} = \frac{16}{24}$
   $+\frac{5 \times 3}{8 \times 3} = \frac{15}{24}$
   $\overline{} \frac{31}{24} = 1\frac{7}{24}$

4. $\frac{3 \times 4}{5 \times 4} = \frac{12}{20}$
   $-\frac{1 \times 5}{4 \times 5} = \frac{5}{20}$
   $\overline{} \frac{7}{20}$

5. $\frac{1 \times 3}{8 \times 3} = \frac{3}{24}$
   $+\frac{2 \times 8}{3 \times 8} = \frac{16}{24}$
   $\overline{} \frac{19}{24}$

6. $\frac{5}{8}$
   $-\frac{1}{8}$
   $\overline{} \frac{4}{8} = \frac{1}{2}$

7. $\frac{2 \times 4}{3 \times 4} = \frac{8}{12}$
   $-\frac{7 \times 1}{12 \times 1} = \frac{7}{12}$
   $\overline{} \frac{1}{12}$

8. $\frac{1}{8}$
   $+\frac{5}{8}$
   $\overline{} \frac{6}{8} = \frac{3}{4}$

9. $\frac{3 \times 4}{5 \times 4} = \frac{12}{20}$
   $+\frac{1 \times 5}{4 \times 5} = \frac{5}{20}$
   $\overline{} \frac{17}{20}$

1. 210   3. $\frac{2}{6} = \frac{1}{3}$
2. 52   4. 51.38

Page 12

Gridlock

×	$\frac{2}{3}$	$\frac{5}{7}$	$\frac{1}{6}$	$\frac{3}{4}$
$\frac{1}{2}$	$\frac{2}{6}=\frac{1}{3}$	$\frac{5}{14}$	$\frac{1}{12}$	$\frac{3}{8}$
$\frac{4}{5}$	$\frac{8}{15}$	$\frac{20}{35}=\frac{4}{7}$	$\frac{4}{30}=\frac{2}{15}$	$\frac{12}{20}=\frac{3}{5}$
$\frac{3}{8}$	$\frac{6}{24}=\frac{1}{4}$	$\frac{15}{56}$	$\frac{3}{48}=\frac{1}{16}$	$\frac{9}{32}$
$\frac{2}{9}$	$\frac{4}{27}$	$\frac{10}{63}$	$\frac{2}{54}=\frac{1}{27}$	$\frac{6}{36}=\frac{1}{6}$

1. $\frac{4}{9}$ 3. 6,000
2. 3.5   4. $\frac{4}{15}$

Page 13

Pyramid Mystery

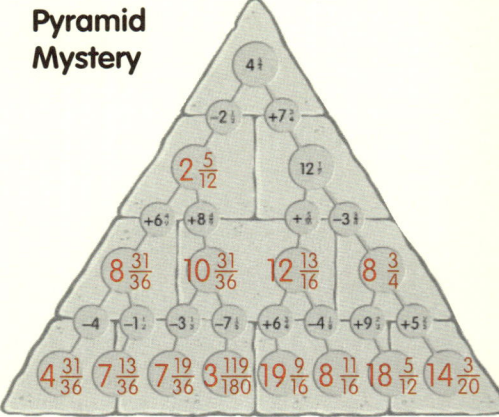

1. .08   3. 1,000,005
2. 51   4. $\frac{6}{9} = \frac{2}{3}$

Page 14

Around Times

$3\frac{2}{3} \times 2\frac{2}{5} = 8\frac{4}{5} \times 3\frac{1}{8} = 27\frac{1}{2} \times \frac{1}{10} =$
$2\frac{3}{4} \times 4\frac{2}{11} = 11\frac{1}{2} \times 1\frac{1}{3} = 15\frac{1}{3} \times 2\frac{4}{23}$
$= 33\frac{1}{3} \times \frac{1}{10} = 3\frac{1}{3} \times 5\frac{1}{4} = 17\frac{1}{2} \times \frac{3}{14}$
$= 3\frac{3}{4} \times 2\frac{2}{7} = 8\frac{4}{7} \times 1\frac{1}{5} = 10\frac{2}{7}$

1. Answers will vary.
2. 140
3. $\frac{7}{24}$ 4. $\frac{2}{5}$

Page 15

Graphic Charts

1. Band
2. Tech Ed.
3. 10%
4. 14%
5. 40 students

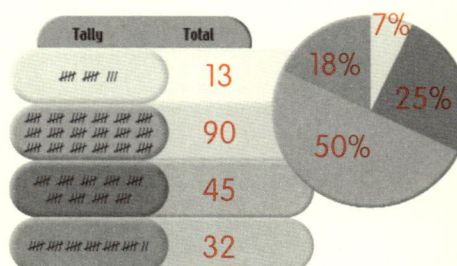

Answers

Math Grade 5

Page 16

Getting Down to Earth

1. .001
2. 111.6
3. 97.2
4. 23.93
5. 1.2
6. .21
7. 365.25

1. 125
2. 8,982
3. $\frac{3}{9} = \frac{1}{3}$
4. 57,600

Page 17

A Square Deal

10.72	1.34	8.04
4.02	6.7	9.38
5.36	12.06	2.68

10.2	1.275	7.65
3.825	6.375	8.925
5.1	11.475	2.55

3.3	8.8	7.7
11	6.6	2.2
5.5	4.4	9.9

1. 28
2. 3
3. 7.2
4. $\frac{5}{6}$

Page 18

Diamonds

1. 0.04 × 5.3 = 0.212
2. 32.6 × 7.51 = 244.826
3. 20.9 × 5.3 = 110.77
4. 0.04 × 7.51 = 0.3004
5. 32.6 × 20.9 = 681.34
6. 7.51 × 5.3 = 39.803
7. 32.6 × 0.04 = 1.304
8. 20.9 × 7.51 = 156.959
9. 5.3 × 32.6 = 172.78

1. $\frac{1}{2}, \frac{5}{8}, \frac{3}{4}$
2. 117
3. 314 cm

Page 19

Read about It

Answers will vary.

1. 9
2. even
3. $\frac{5}{12} + \frac{1}{6} = \frac{7}{12}$
4. 98.65

Page 20

The Great Divide

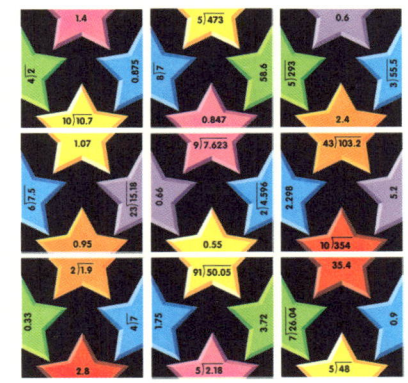

1. 33
2. 6
3. $\frac{5}{8} = \frac{25}{40}$
4. 81 mm²

Page 21

A Solid Workout

1. V = 64 mm³
   SA = 96 mm²
2. V = 176.4 cm³
   SA = 226.8 cm²
3. V = 143.5 km³
   SA = 342 km²
4. V = 125 m³
   SA = 123 m²
5. V = 900 m³
   SA = 650 m²
6. V = 1280 cm³
   SA = 736 cm²

1. .25
2. 3.43
3. 27 m³
4. 4

Page 22

FUNctions

Add 4.5	Multiply by $\frac{1}{2}$
7.5	6
7.2	$\frac{2}{18} = \frac{1}{9}$
10.75	$\frac{8}{10} = \frac{4}{5}$
4.58	2.15

Divide by 5	Multiply by 2 then multiply by π
73	62.8 m
16.8	12.56 m
2.47	37.68 m
182.8	251.2 m

1. 7,799
2. <
3. 18.00
4. $\frac{11}{3} \times \frac{2}{1} = \frac{22}{3} = 7\frac{1}{3}$

Answers

MATH Grade 5

Page 23

Have a Ball

W = 2	Z = 5	B = 4
Q = 1	W = 8	V = 2
L = 2	N = 3	Z = 2
M = 3	J = 0	K = 7
N = 0	H = 7	A = 0
X = 9	Y = 3	S = 9
D = 7	B = 4	M = 6
F = 9	X = 1	I = 4
G = 3	M = 8	V = 9
		A = 8
		L = 9
		R = 2
		P = 1

1. 81, 243, 729
2. .37
3. forty five million, six hundred seventy thousand, three
4. 4

Page 24

It's Magic

2	9	4
7	5	3
6	1	8

1. 5 : 4
2. 5 : 4
3. 4 : 4
4. 2 : 2
5. 2 : 9
6. 3 : 4
7. 3 : 9

1. 21.84 cm^2
2. $\frac{2}{3}$
3. five and eighty seven hundredths
4. 13

Page 25

In the Shade

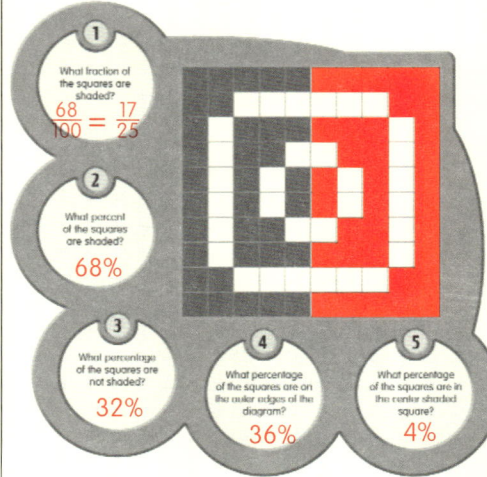

1. $\frac{68}{100} = \frac{17}{25}$
2. 68%
3. 32%
4. 36%
5. 4%

1. February, March, April
2. $\frac{5}{8} - \frac{1}{6} = \frac{11}{24}$
3. 80% = $\frac{4}{5}$

Page 26

Flip Over Percents

For 1 player:

(In any order)

50% = $\frac{1}{2}$ 0.25 = 25%

80% = $\frac{4}{5}$ 10% = 0.1

0.6 = 60% $\frac{3}{4}$ = 0.75

$\frac{3}{10}$ = 30%   17% = $\frac{17}{100}$

For 2 players:

Answers may vary.

1. 16, 25, 36
2. 14
3. 3,045
4. Odd

Page 27

Do Get Cross

Crossword grid with answers:
a. 1 5 b. 2   c. 2 2 d. 4
   2   e. 4 5 0   f. 3 9
g. 1 h. 8 0   i. 4 5 j.
            1   k. 3 1 3
   m. 9 3 n. 8   5   9
o. 1   4   p. 6 0
q. 5 r. 1   0
s. 7 0 0   t. 2 9

1. 10
2. 63
3. 24
4. 60 cm^3

Page 28

Flippety-doo-dah

1. Penny
   There are more pennies than any other coin.
2. Quarter
   There are fewer quarters than any other coin.
3. $.90

Tally

Answers may vary.

Total

Answers may vary.

Probability

Nickels:
5 ÷ 19 = .26 = 26%

Dimes:
3 ÷ 19 = .16 = 16%

Quarters:
1 ÷ 19 = .05 = 5%

Graphic Charts

Skill: Circle graphs

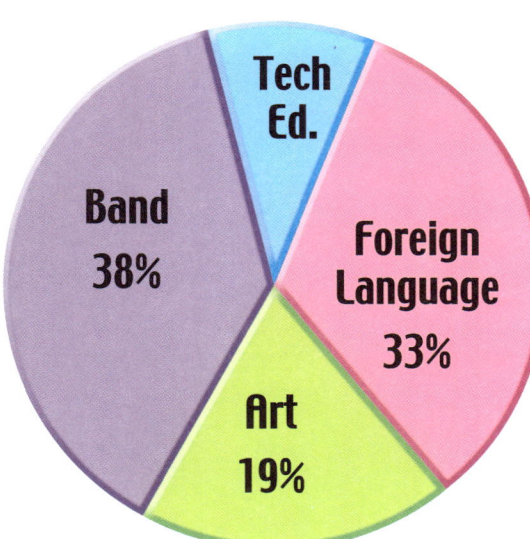

A group of students was surveyed about their elective courses. Use the graph to answer the questions.

1. Which elective was most popular? _____
2. Which elective was least popular? _____
3. What percent took Tech Ed.? _____
4. What is the difference between the percentage of students taking Foreign Language and those taking Art?
_____
5. If 80 students took Band, how many students took Art? _____

A group of students was surveyed about favorite colors. Fill in the circle graph based on the information in the table.

Tally	Total
𝍢 𝍢 ||| (yellow)	
𝍢 𝍢 𝍢 𝍢 𝍢 𝍢 𝍢 𝍢 𝍢 𝍢 𝍢 𝍢 𝍢 𝍢 𝍢 𝍢 𝍢 𝍢 (blue)	
𝍢 𝍢 𝍢 𝍢 𝍢 𝍢 𝍢 𝍢 𝍢 (red)	
𝍢 𝍢 𝍢 𝍢 𝍢 𝍢 𝍢 || (green)	

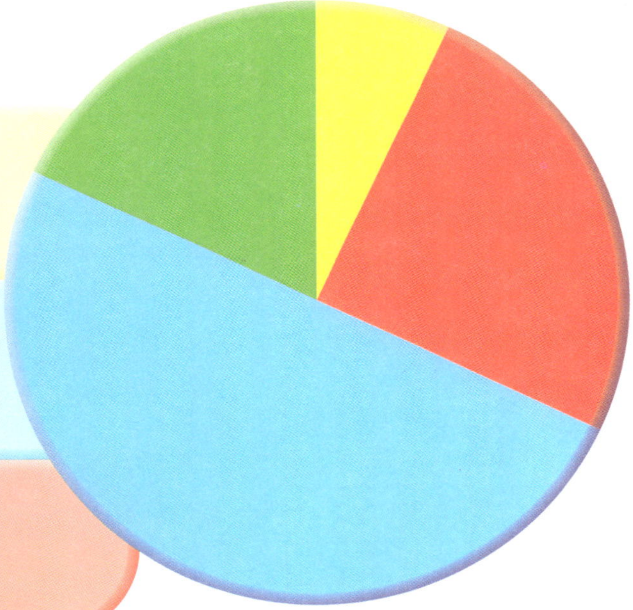

Challenge! Figure the percentages for each section. Add up the total number of tallys. Divide that number into the tallies in each color group.

Getting Down to Earth

Skill: Decimal place value

Use digits to write the numbers in decimal form after each statement. Express the fractions as decimals. Then place the number in the correct spot in the puzzle grid below.

1. Only one thousandth of all the earth's moisture is in the air. _____

2. The tallest tree is one hundred eleven and six tenths meters high. _____

3. Ninety-seven and two tenths of all water on earth is in the oceans. _____

4. The earth rotates once every twenty-three and ninety-three hundredths hours. _____

5. Each year, the Atlantic Ocean increases in width by one and two tenths inches. _____

6. Twenty-one hundredths of the earth's atmosphere is oxygen. _____

7. The earth takes three hundred sixty-five and twenty-five hundredths days to orbit the sun. _____

1. One bus holds 25 people. 5 buses hold _____ people.

2. 2,543 + _____ = 11,525

3. $\frac{2}{9} + \frac{1}{9} =$ _____

4. Write fifty-seven thousand six hundred in digits. _____

A Square Deal

Skill: Adding and subtracting decimals

A magic square is a square where the numbers in each row, column, and diagonal add up to the same sum. Fill in the blanks to make each of these a magic square.

10.72	1.34	8.04
	6.7	

		7.65
	6.375	
5.1		2.55

3.3		
	11	6.6
5.5		

1. 902 − 874 = _____

2. The GCF of 15 and 24 is _____.

3. 2.4 × 3 = _____

4. $\frac{1}{2} + \frac{1}{3}$ = _____

17

Math Skillbook

©2000 TREND enterprises, Inc.

Diamonds

Skill: Multiplying decimals

Use the numbers in the diagram to solve each problem.

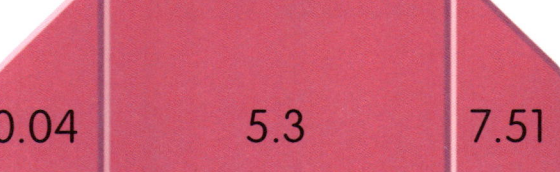

1. ◁ = _____
   ☐ = _____
   × _____

2. △ = _____
   ▷ = _____
   × _____

3. ▽ = _____
   ☐ = _____
   × _____

4. ◁ = _____
   ▷ = _____
   × _____

5. △ = _____
   ▽ = _____
   × _____

6. ▷ = _____
   ☐ = _____
   × _____

7. △ = _____
   ◁ = _____
   × _____

8. ▽ = _____
   ▷ = _____
   × _____

9. ☐ = _____
   △ = _____
   × _____

Mind Stretchers

1. $\frac{1}{8}$, $\frac{1}{4}$, $\frac{3}{8}$, ____, ____, ____

2. $\frac{585}{5}$ = ____

3. Find the circumference of a circle with a radius of 50 cm to the nearest whole number.
   _____

18

Math Skillbook   ©2000 TREND enterprises, Inc.

Read about It

Skills: Collecting and analyzing data, Predicting outcomes

Which letter of the alphabet do you think is used most often? ____ Least often? ____
Let's find out if your predictions are correct!

Choose a paragraph of at least 25 words from a newspaper or your favorite book. Use the table to keep track of the use of each letter in the paragraph.

Letter	Tally	Total
A		
B		
C		
D		
E		
F		
G		
H		
I		
J		
K		
L		
M		

Letter	Tally	Total
N		
O		
P		
Q		
R		
S		
T		
U		
V		
W		
X		
Y		
Z		

Were your predictions correct? _____

Do you think one sample is enough? Try another sample from a different source. Use a different color pen or pencil so you can mark tallies on the same table.

Mind Stretchers

1. $\frac{81}{9} =$ ____

2. An odd number times an even number = an _____ number.

3. $\frac{}{12} + \frac{1}{6} = \frac{7}{12}$

4. Round 98.654 to the nearest hundredth. _____

The Great Divide

Skill: Dividing decimals

Cut the diagram into the 9 cards. Match the problems to the correct answers. When you are done, the cards will form a square again.

remember: Complete and check the previous page before cutting this page.

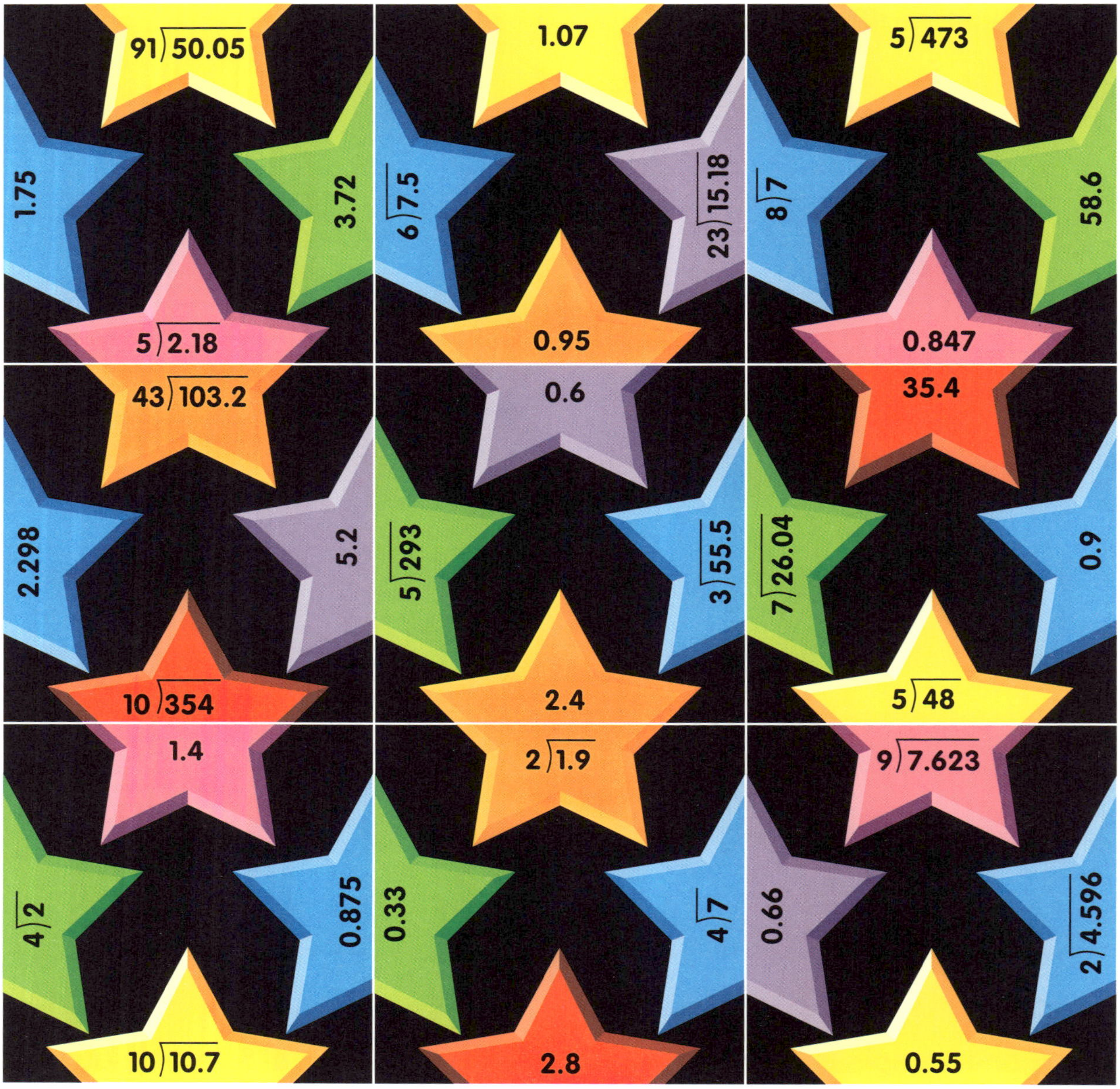

91)50.05	1.07	5)473
1.75 · 3.72	6)7.5 · 23)15.18	8)7 · 58.6
5)2.18	0.95	0.847
43)103.2	0.6	35.4
2.298 · 5.2	5)293 · 3)55.5	7)26.04 · 0.9
10)354	2.4	5)48
1.4	2)1.9	9)7.623
4)2 · 0.875	0.33 · 4)7	0.66 · 2)4.596
10)10.7	2.8	0.55

1. 11 × 12 = 4 × ___

2. The average of 4, 6, and 8 is ___.

3. $\frac{5}{8} = \frac{}{40}$

4. The area of a 9 mm square is ___.

20

A Solid Workout

Skills: Volume, Surface area

Find the surface area and volume of each rectangular prism.

Remember: Surface area is the sum of the areas of all sides. Volume is length x width x height.

1. 4 mm, 4 mm

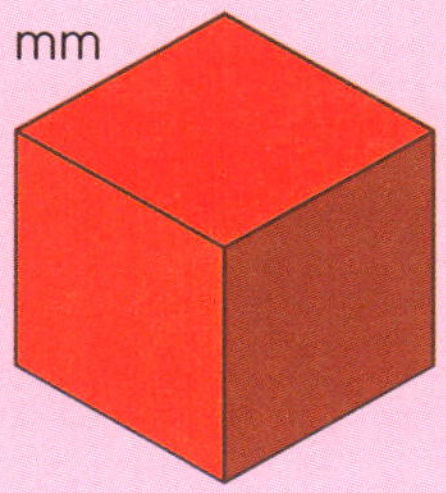

V = _____
SA = _____

2. 4.2 cm, 3 cm, 14 cm

V = _____
SA = _____

3. 20.5 km, 7 km, 1 km

V = _____
SA = _____

4. 5 m, 3 m, 3 m, 3 m, 5 m, 5 m

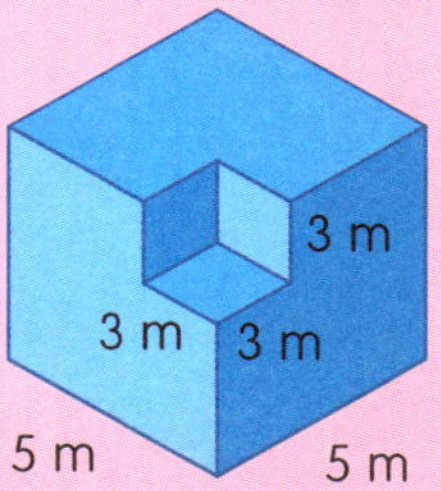

V = _____
SA = _____

5. 20 m, 5 m, 9 m

V = _____
SA = _____

6. 8 cm, 10 cm, 16 cm

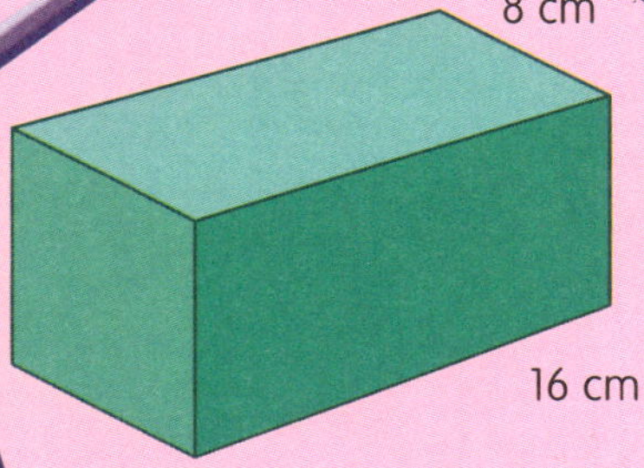

V = _____
SA = _____

1. Convert $\frac{1}{4}$ to a decimal. _____
2. 4.9 x 0.7 = _____
3. The volume of a 3 m cube is _____.
4. An octagon has ____ more sides than a trapezoid.

21

Math Skillbook

©2000 TREND enterprises, Inc.

FUNctions

Skill: Algebra functions

For each function, input the given numbers and operations to get the correct output answers.

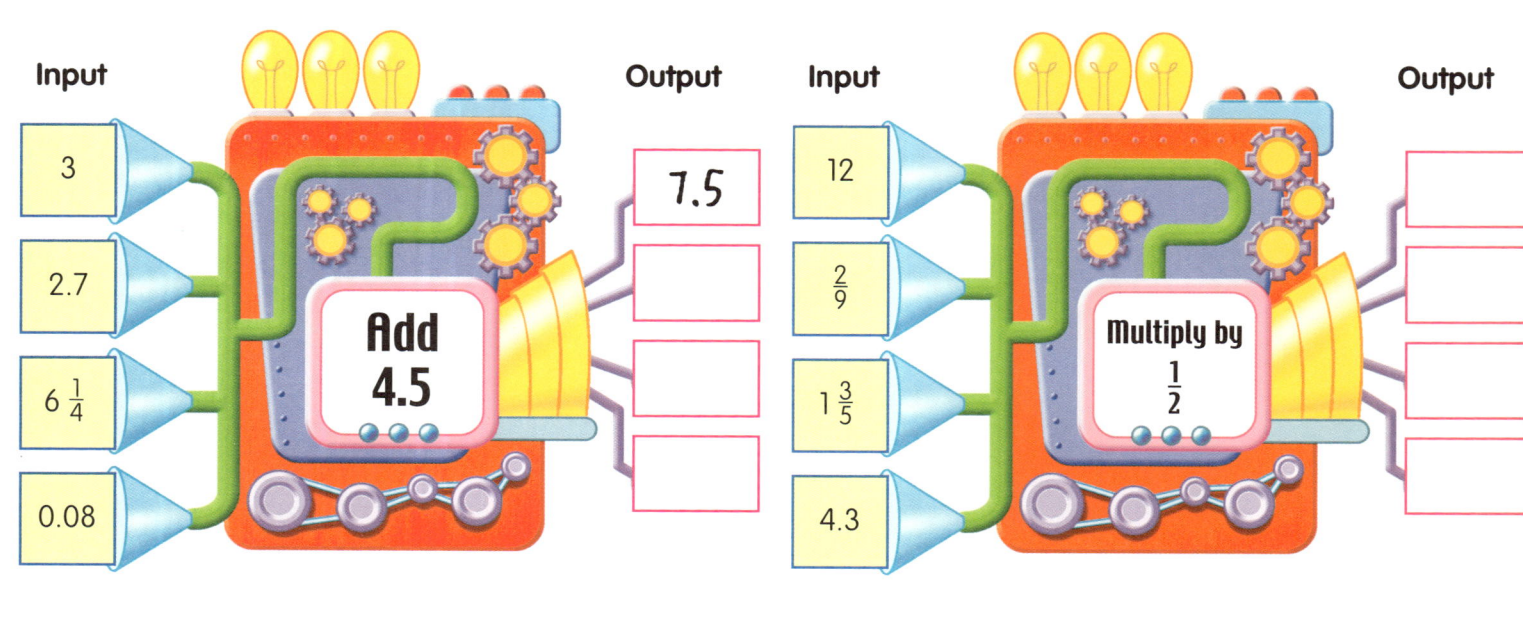

Function 1 — Add 4.5
- Input: 3 → Output: 7.5
- Input: 2.7 → Output: ___
- Input: 6 1/4 → Output: ___
- Input: 0.08 → Output: ___

Function 2 — Multiply by 1/2
- Input: 12 → Output: ___
- Input: 2/9 → Output: ___
- Input: 1 3/5 → Output: ___
- Input: 4.3 → Output: ___

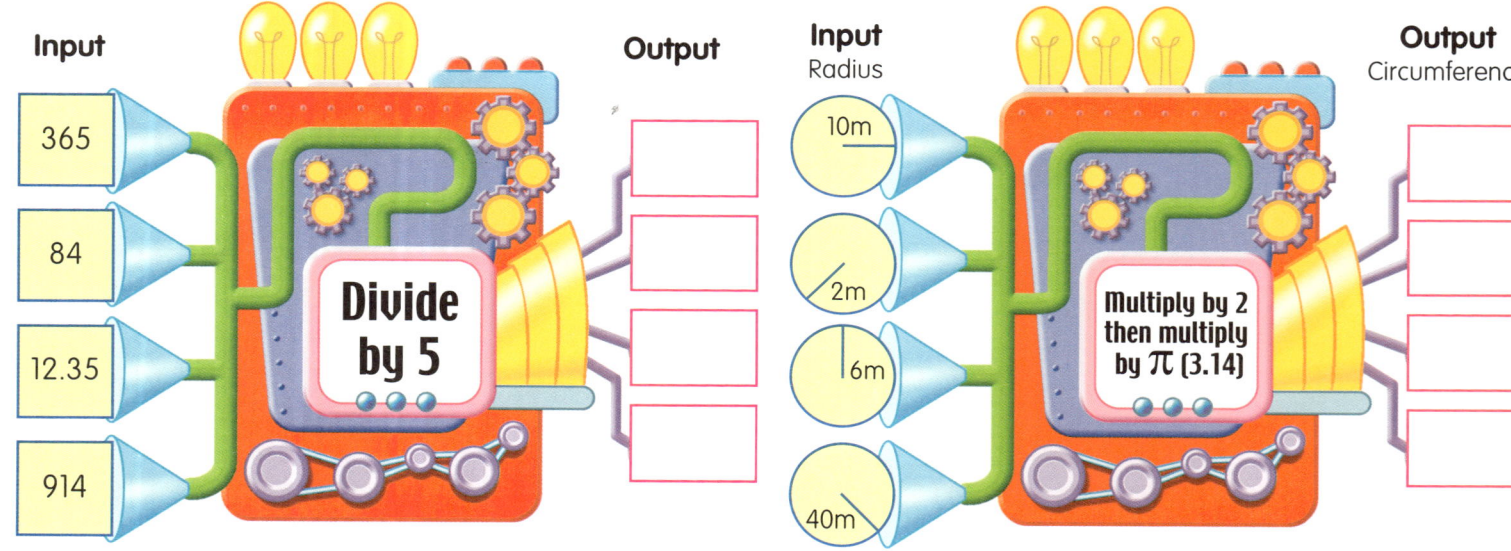

Function 3 — Divide by 5
- Input: 365 → Output: ___
- Input: 84 → Output: ___
- Input: 12.35 → Output: ___
- Input: 914 → Output: ___

Function 4 — Multiply by 2 then multiply by π (3.14)
Input: Radius / Output: Circumference
- 10m → ___
- 2m → ___
- 6m → ___
- 40m → ___

1. 8,000 − 201 = _____
2. $\frac{2}{5}$ (> <) 0.6
3. $4.50/week savings = $_____/month
4. $\frac{11}{3} \times 2 =$ _____

Math Skillbook

©2000 TREND enterprises, Inc.

Have a Ball

Skill: Algebra variables

Solve the problems to find the values of the letters.

```
  7 W 8        W = ____
+ 5 1 Q        Q = ____
-------
  1 L 3 9      L = ____
```

```
  B 3 1        B = ____
+ 3 9 V        V = ____
-------
  8 Z 3        Z = ____
```

```
  Z 7 W        Z = ____
+ 1 N 8        W = ____
-------
  7 1 6        N = ____
```

```
    5 3 8      K = ____
+ 3 K A        A = ____
-------
  S 0 8        S = ____
```

```
  6 5 M        M = ____
+ 3 N 4        N = ____
-------
  X 5 7        X = ____
```

```
  J 6 8        J = ____
+ 1 H 5        H = ____
-------
  2 4 Y        Y = ____
```

```
  6 0 M        M = ____
+ 3 1 2        I = ____
-------
  V 4 8        V = ____
```

```
  3 D 4        D = ____
+ F 8 9        F = ____
-------
  1 3 6 G      G = ____
```

```
  7 B 5        B = ____
+ 1 3 X        X = ____
-------
  M 7 6        M = ____
```

```
    9 4 5      A = ____
+ 2 A L        L = ____
-------
  P R 3 4      R = ____
               P = ____
```

Mind Stretchers

1. 1, 3, 9, 27, ____, ____, ____

2. 9.25 ÷ 25 = ____

3. Write 45,670,003 in words.
____

4. The GCF of 36 and 8 is ____.

It's Magic

Skill: Ratio

Ratio can be written in three different ways   **4 to 5**   **4 : 5**   **4/5**

A magic square is a square where the numbers in each row, column, and diagonal add up to the same sum. Fill in the blanks to make this a magic square.

2	9	4
		3

Use the numbers in the magic square to find the ratios.

 Odd numbers to even numbers.
_____

 Prime numbers to composite numbers.
_____

 Numbers < 5 to numbers > 5.
_____

 Numbers that begin with the letter f to numbers that begin with the letter t.
_____

 Multiples of 4 to all the numbers.
_____

 Multiples of 3 to multiples of 2.
_____

 Numbers that are perfect squares (i.e. 25 = 5 x 5. 25 is a perfect square) to all the numbers. _____

1. The area of a 2.6 cm x 8.4 cm rectangle = _____
2. $\frac{2}{3} \times 1 =$ _____

3. Write 5.87 in words. _____

4. If 4 mips = 52 bips, then 1 mip = _____ bips.

Math Skillbook   ©2000 TREND enterprises, Inc.

In the Shade

Skill: Percentages

Complete the squares diagram so that the right side is a mirror image of the left side. Then answer the questions.

1 What fraction of the squares are shaded?
_____

2 What percent of the squares are shaded?
_____

3 What percentage of the squares are not shaded?
_____

4 What percentage of the squares are on the outer edges of the diagram?
_____

5 What percentage of the squares are in the center shaded square?
_____

1. Name three consecutive months that usually total 89 days _____, _____, _____.

2. $\frac{5}{8} - \frac{1}{6} =$ _____

3. $80\% = \frac{}{5}$

Math Skillbook

©2000 TREND enterprises, Inc.

Flip Over Percents

Skill: Equivalent decimals, fractions, and percents

Cut out the 16 cards to play one or both of these games.

For 1 player:

Shuffle the cards and spread them out, face down. Turn two over at a time to find a match of equivalent numbers. If they don't match, return them to the face down position and try again.

For 2 players:

Shuffle the cards and deal 8 to each player. Players lay cards face down in front of themselves. Each player turns over a card. The larger value takes both.

If there is a tie, each player turns over another card. The larger value takes all 4 cards. Play continues until one player has all the cards.

remember: Complete and check the previous page before cutting this page.

Cards:
- 60%
- 50%
- 0.25
- 80%
- 10%
- 0.6
- 3/4
- 3/10
- 17%
- 0.75
- 4/5
- 1/2
- 0.1
- 30%
- 17/100
- 25%

Mind Stretchers

1. 1, 4, 9, ___, ___, ___

2. $4\frac{1}{2} + 9\frac{1}{2} =$ _____

3. 145 x 21 = _____

4. An odd number times an odd number = an _____ number.

Do Get Cross

Skill: Finding percentages

Find the percent of the numbers to fill in the "crossnumber" puzzle.

ACROSS

a. 50% of 304
c. 25% of 896
e. 100% of 450
f. 75% of 52
g. 25% of 720
i. 45% of 100
k. 50% of 626
m. 100% of 938
p. 75% of 80
q. 25% of 204
s. 50% of 1400
t. 29% of 100

DOWN

a. 25% of 484
b. 75% of 320
c. 75% of 272
d. 25% of 172
h. 100% of 819
j. 50% of 1070
l. 50% of 780
n. 84% of 100
o. 25% of 628
p. 75% of 812
r. 10% of 100

1. The product of the first 5 prime numbers = _____
2. 106 − y = 43   y = _____
3. 840 ÷ 35 = _____
4. The volume of a 3 cm × 4 cm × 5 cm box = _____

Flippety-doo-dah

Skill: Probability

Place 1 quarter, 3 dimes, 5 nickels, and 10 pennies in a bag or sock. Use the bag or sock to answer the questions.

1 If you reach in and pull out one coin without looking, which coin are you most likely to pick? _____

Why? _____
_____

2 Which coin are you least likely to pick? _____

Why? _____
_____

3 What is the total value of the coins in the sock? _____

4 Reach in and pull out one coin without looking. Mark the result in the table. Put the coin back and do the activity 24 more times.

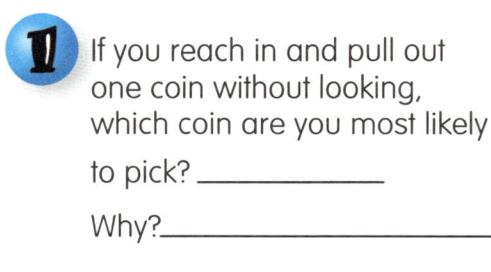

	Pennies	Nickels	Dimes	Quarters
Tally				
Total				

Write the probability of picking each coin.

Probability	10 (# of pennies) ÷ 19 (total # of coins) = .526 = 53%			

Do the Coin Flip

Place 3 nickels and 3 pennies on the coin flip strip. Now switch the pennies and nickels using these rules.

1 Nickels can only move to the right. Pennies can only move to the left.

2 No space can have 2 coins on it at once.

3 A coin can flip over another coin, but only one at a time.

Math Skillbook

©2000 TREND enterprises, Inc.